Dimensions
COLORING BOOK

John Wik

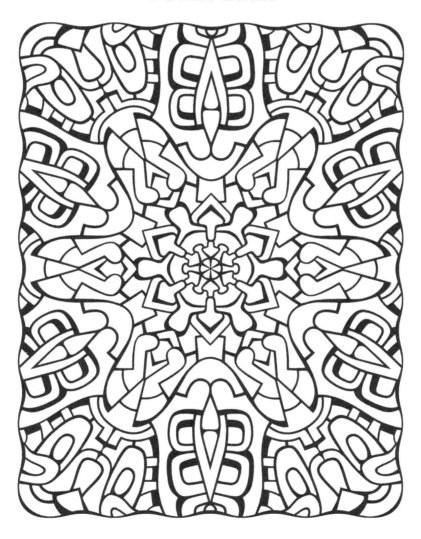

DOVER PUBLICATIONS, INC.
MINEOLA, NEW YORK

In this latest edition to Dover's *Creative Haven* series for the experienced colorist, big, beautiful, abstract mandala designs will transport you to another dimension. The bold yet detailed patterns are perfect for experimentation with different media and color techniques, and the perforated pages make displaying finished work easy!

Bibliographical Note
Dimensions Coloring Book is a new work,
first published by Dover Publications, Inc., in 2015.

International Standard Book Number
ISBN-13: 978-0-486-79539-3
ISBN-10: 0-486-79539-X

Manufactured in the United States by LSC Communications
79539X06   2019
www.doverpublications.com

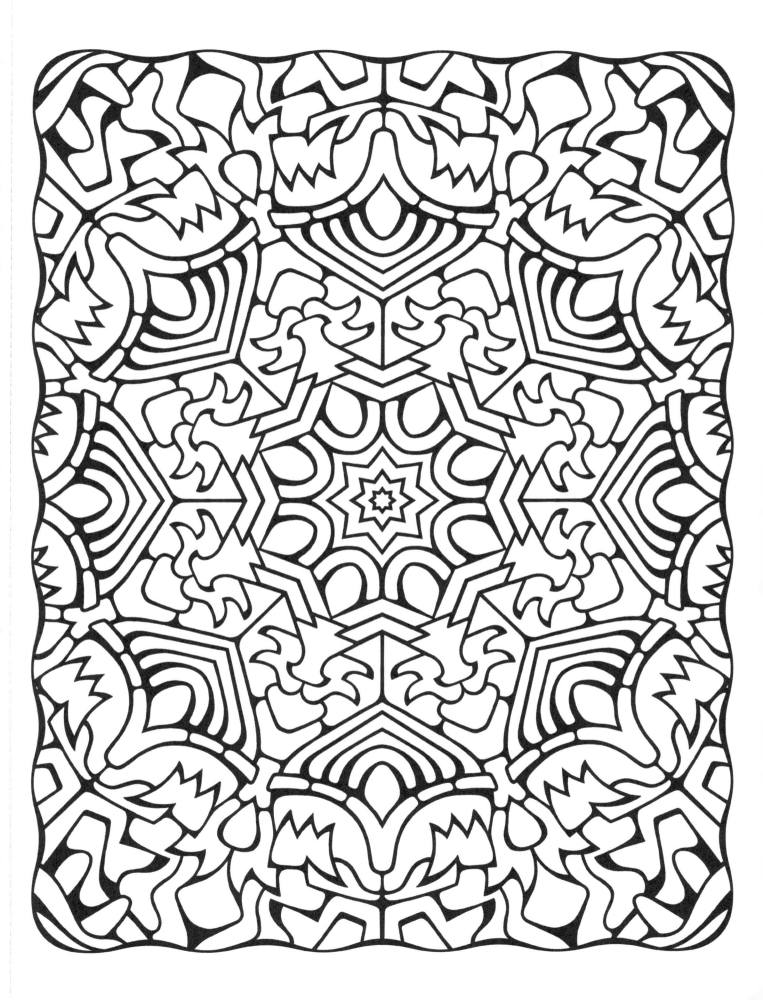

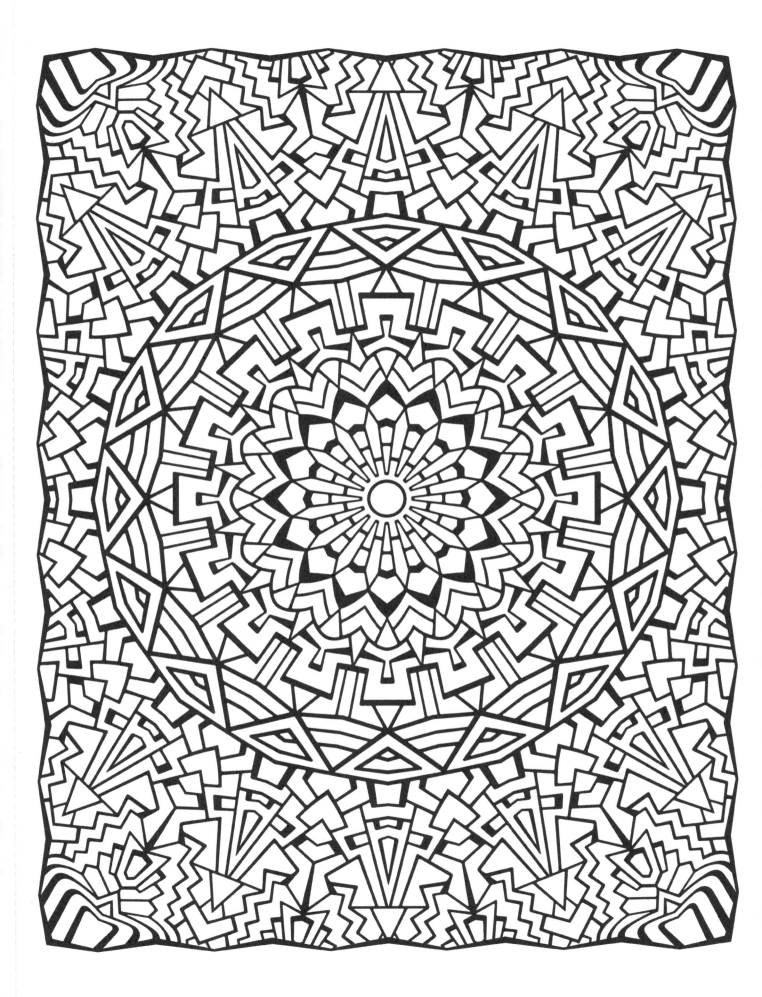

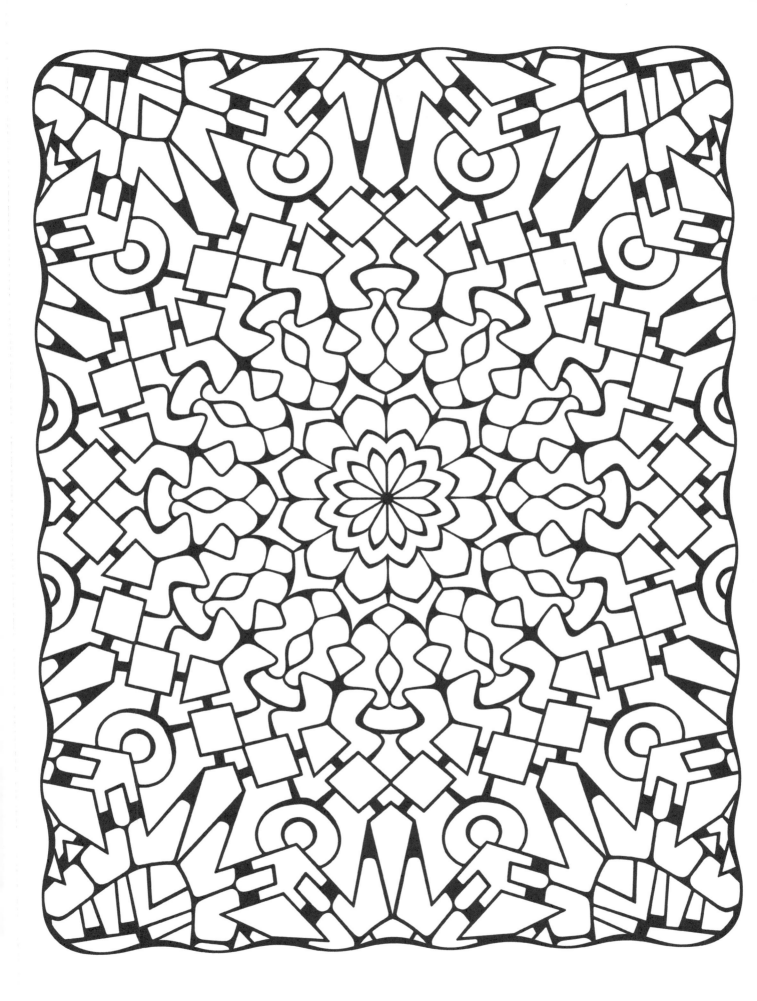

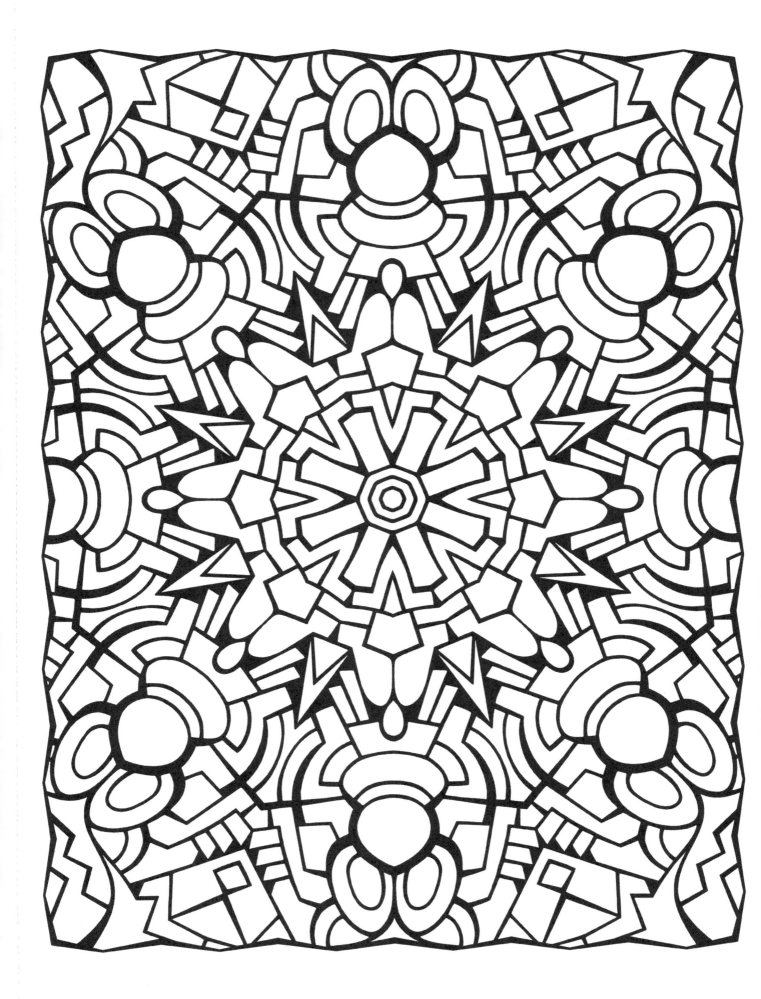

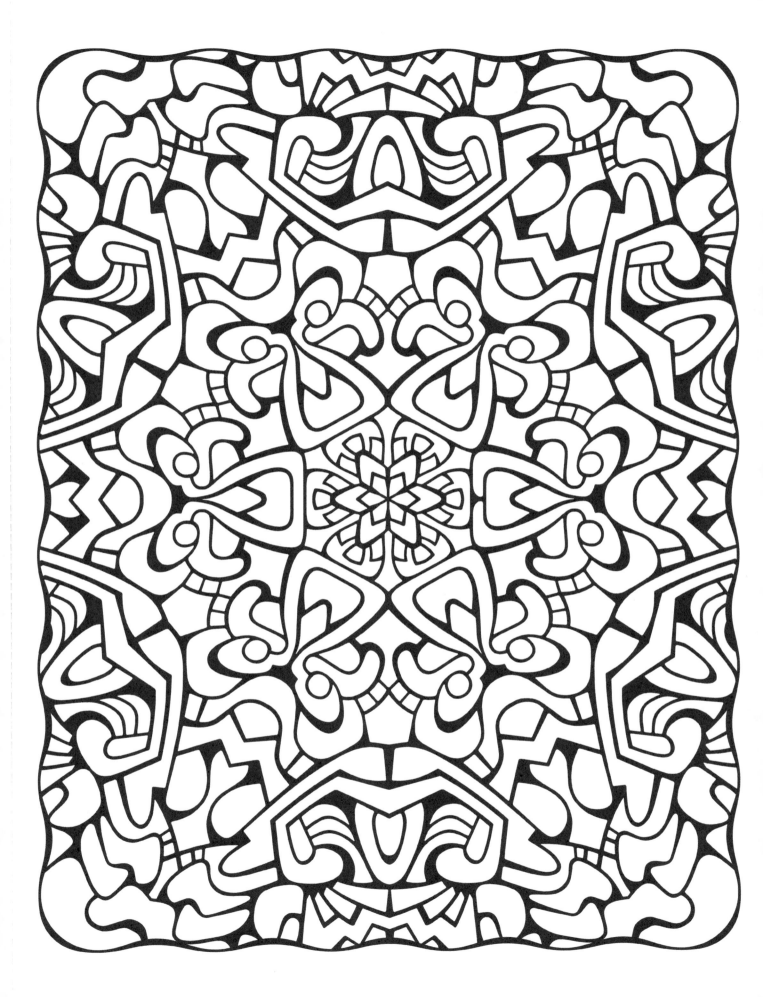

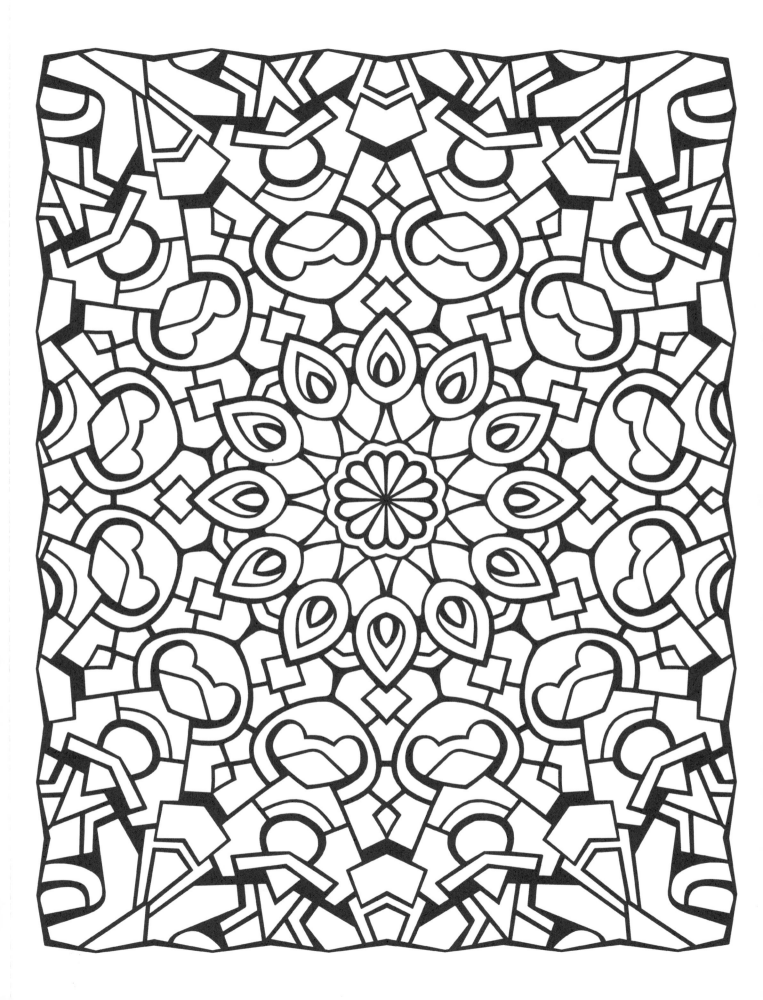

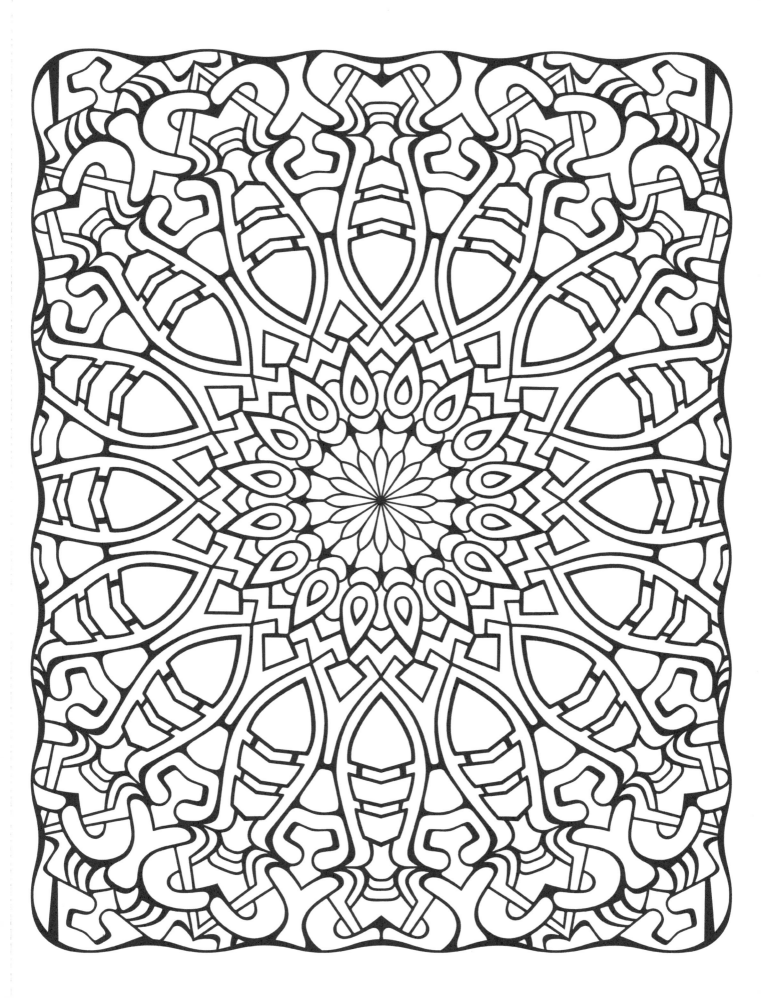

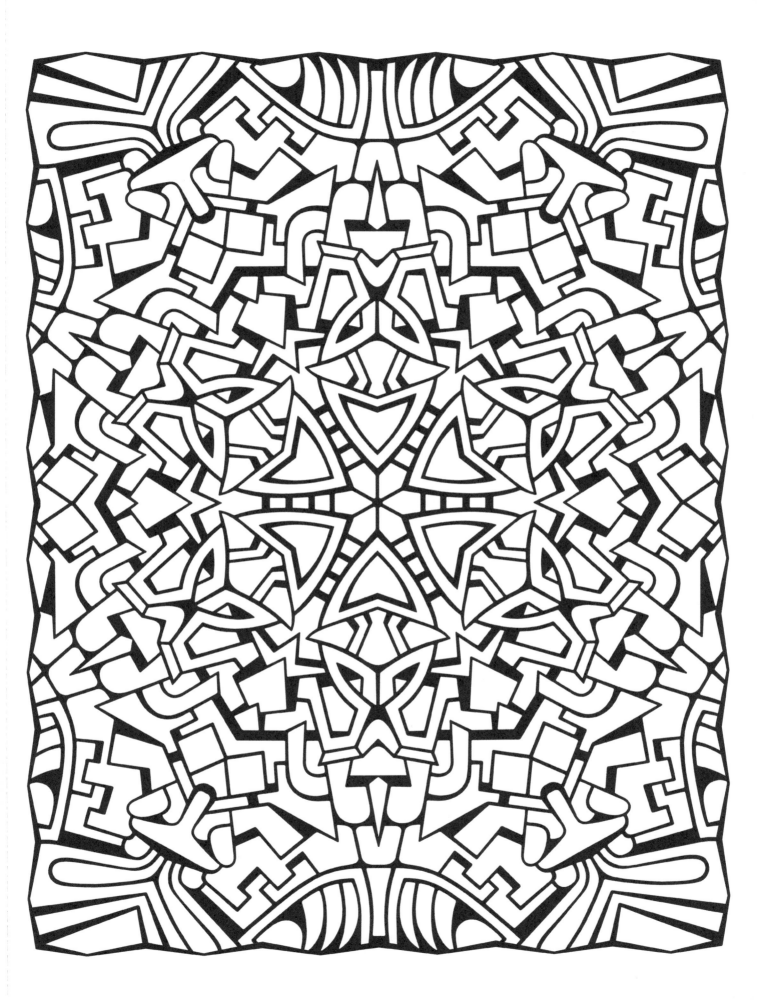

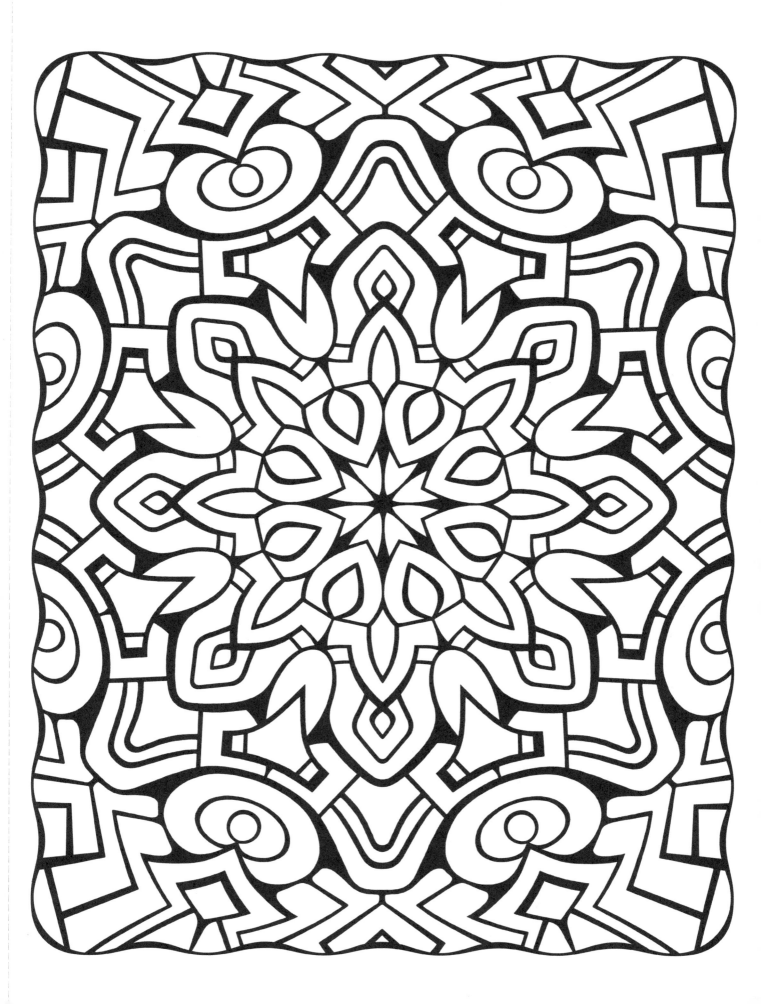

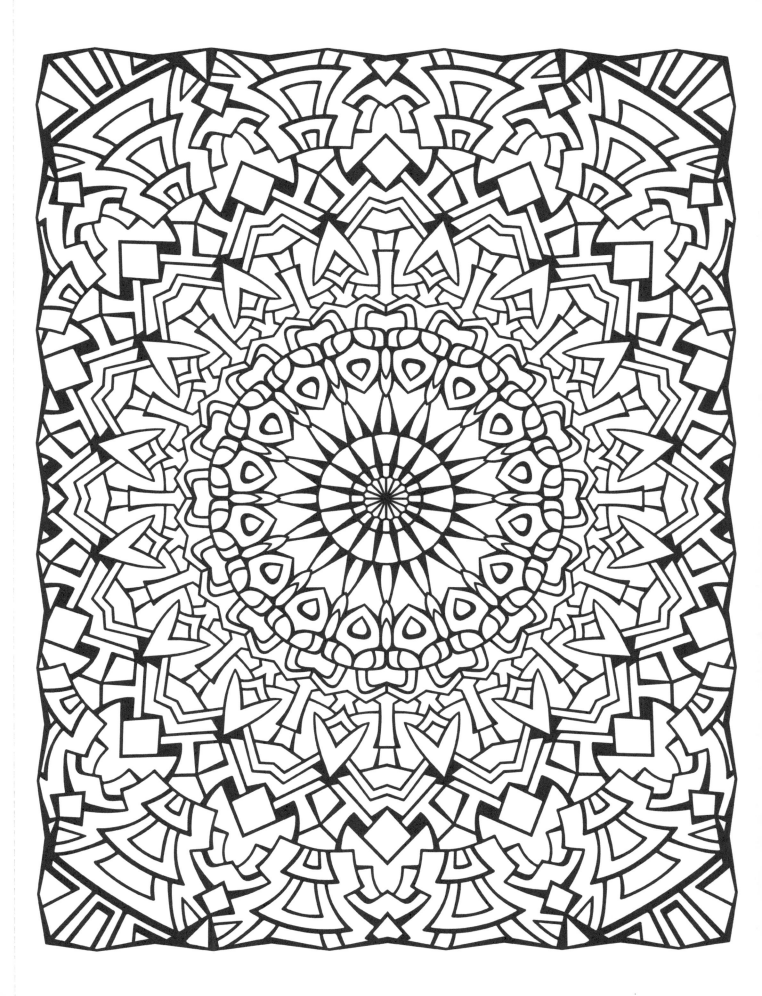

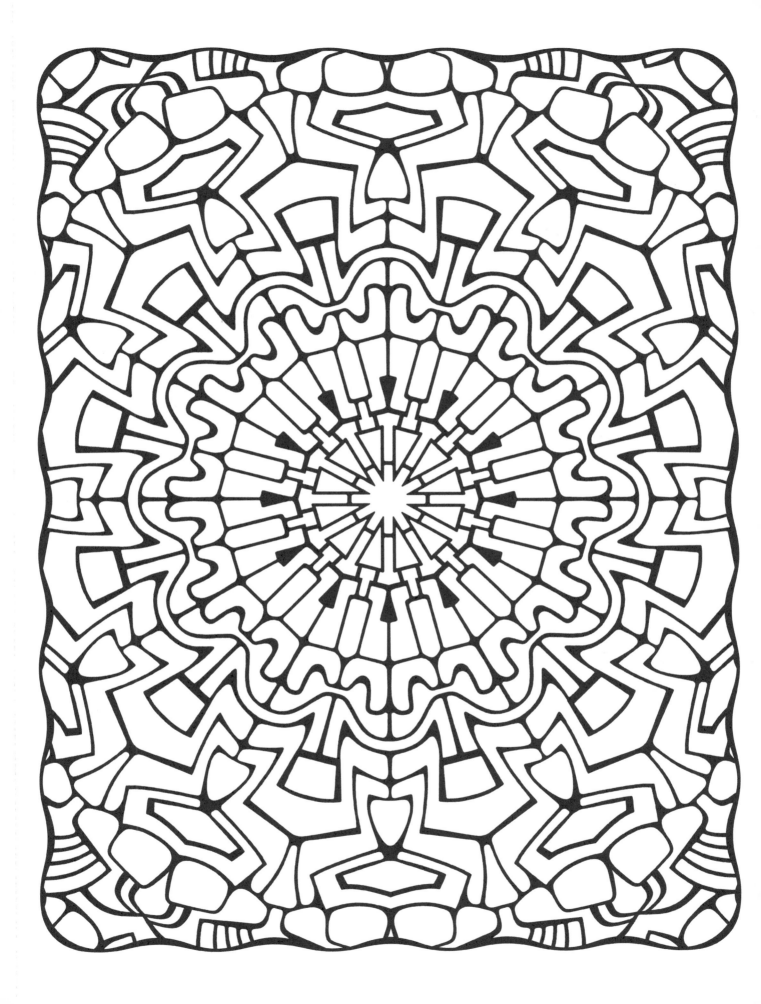

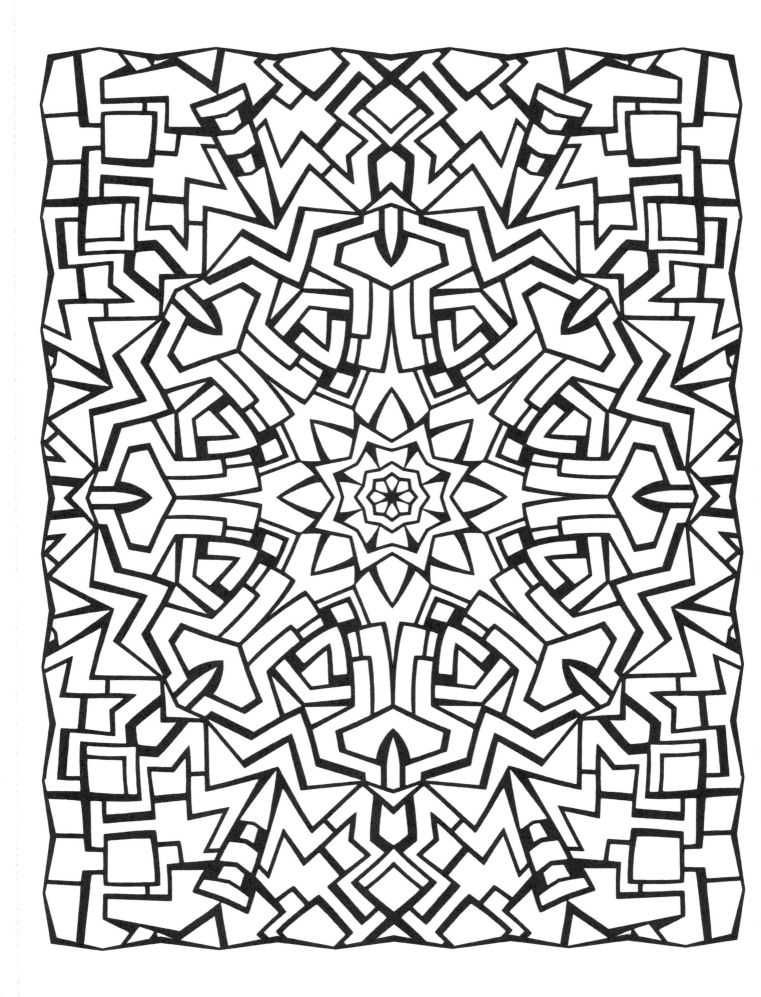

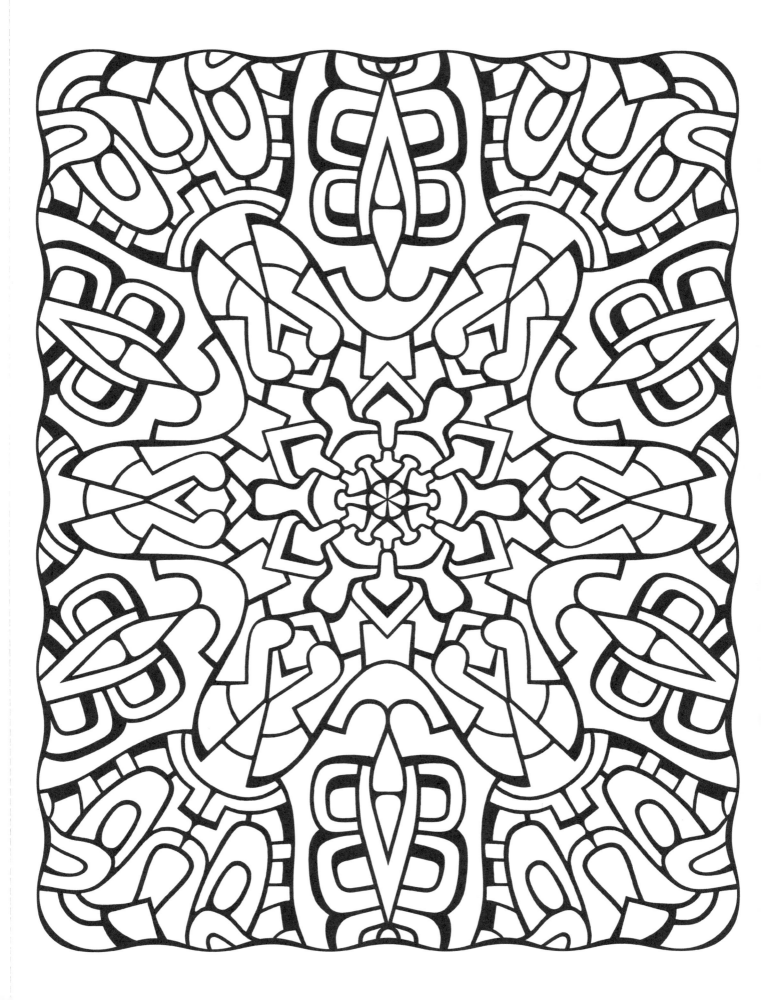

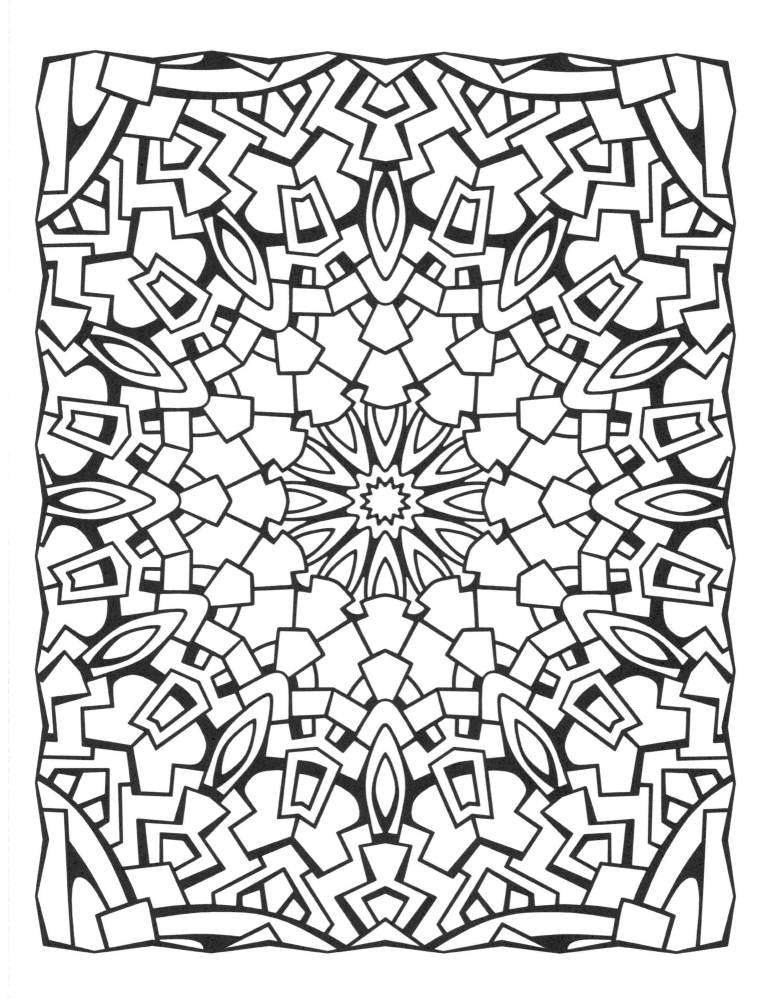

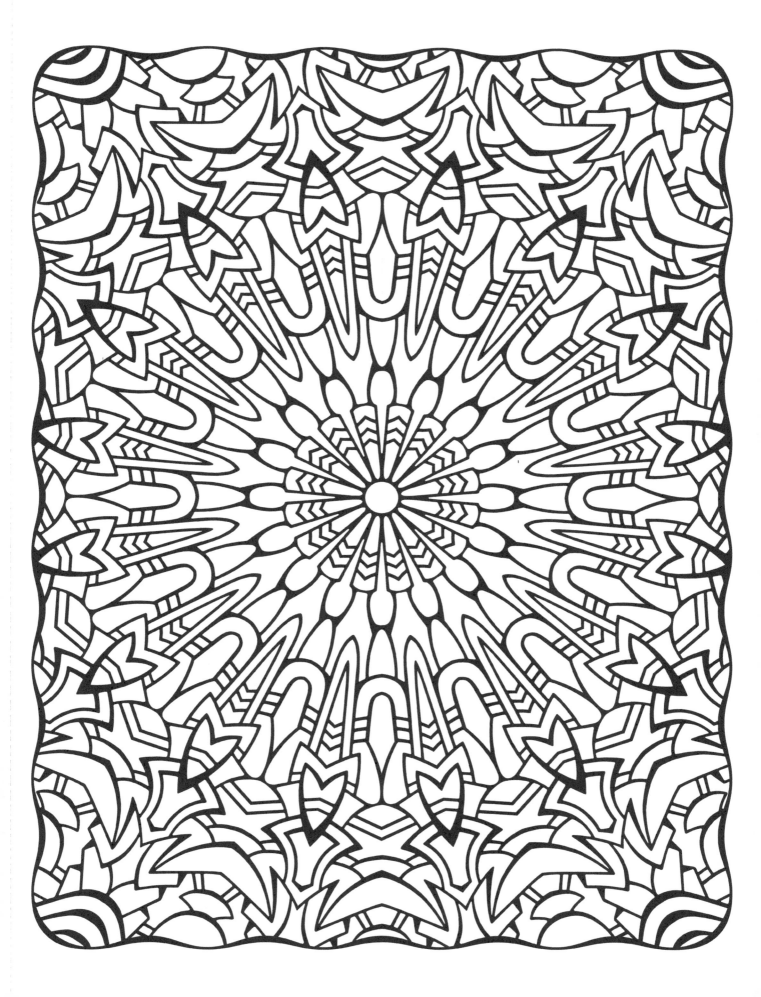

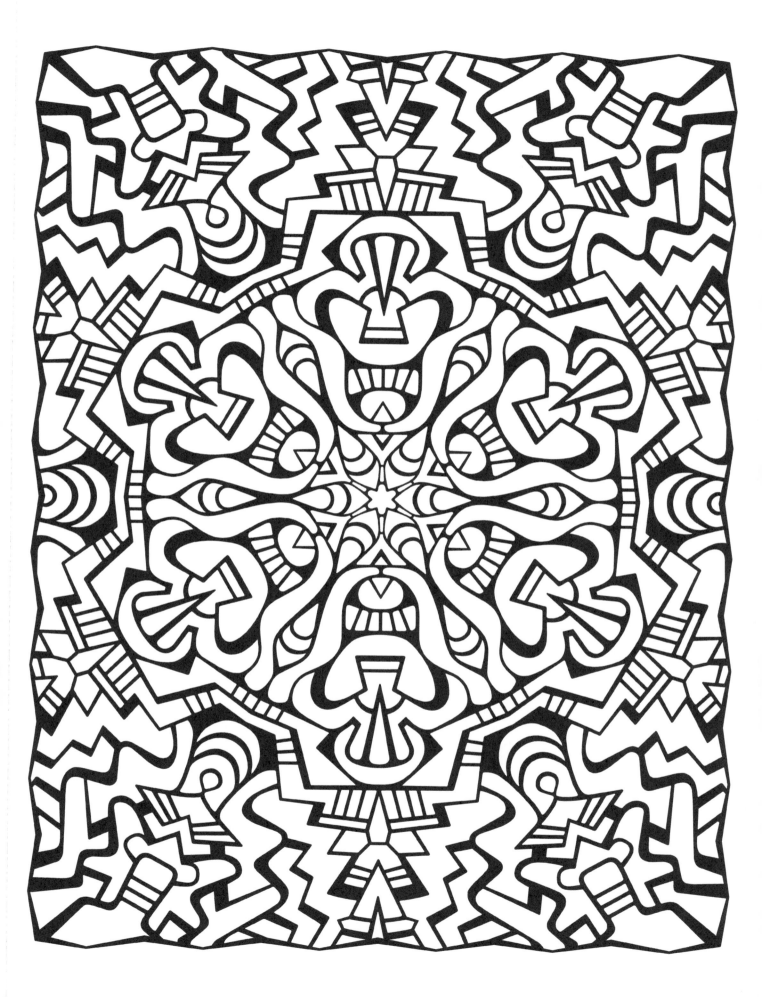

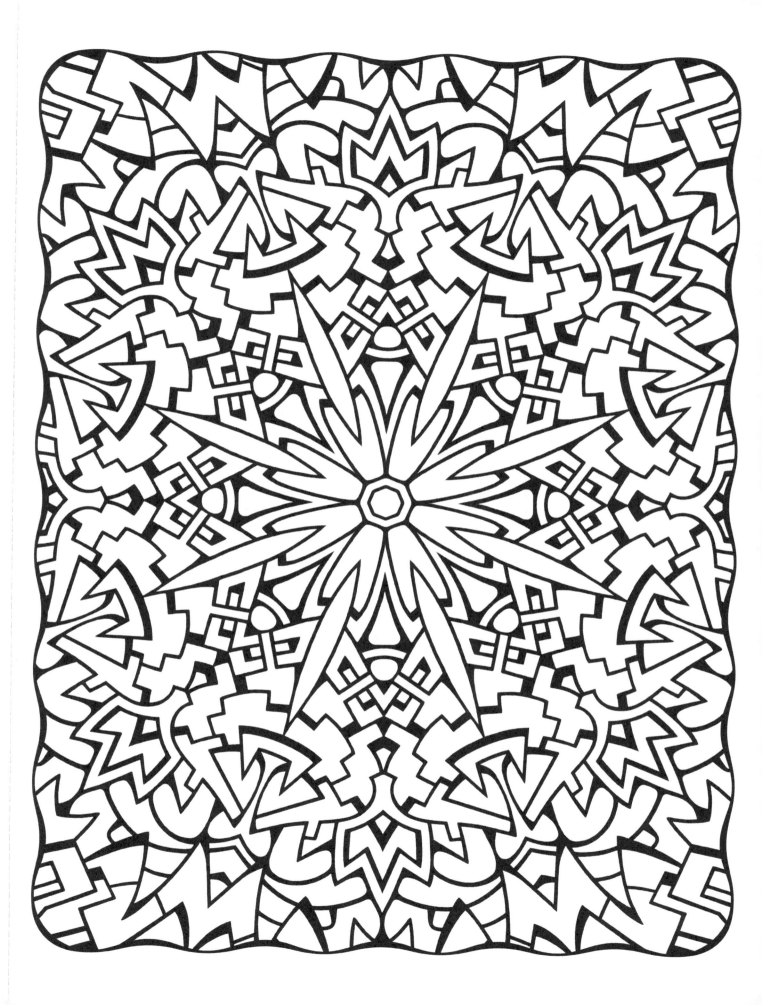

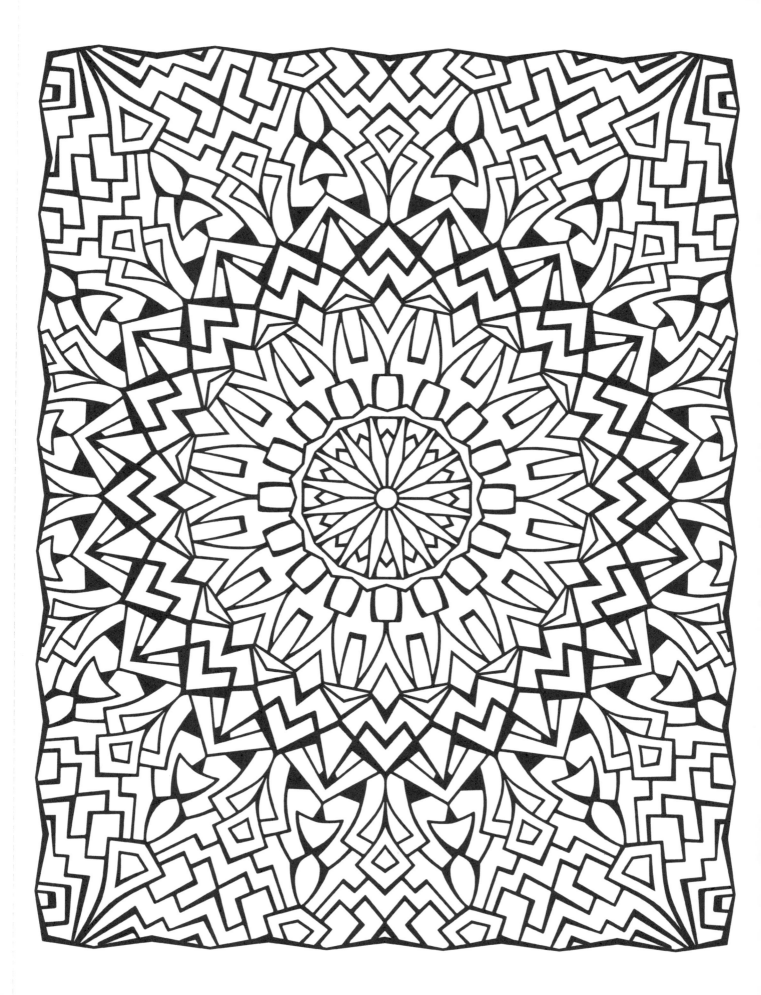

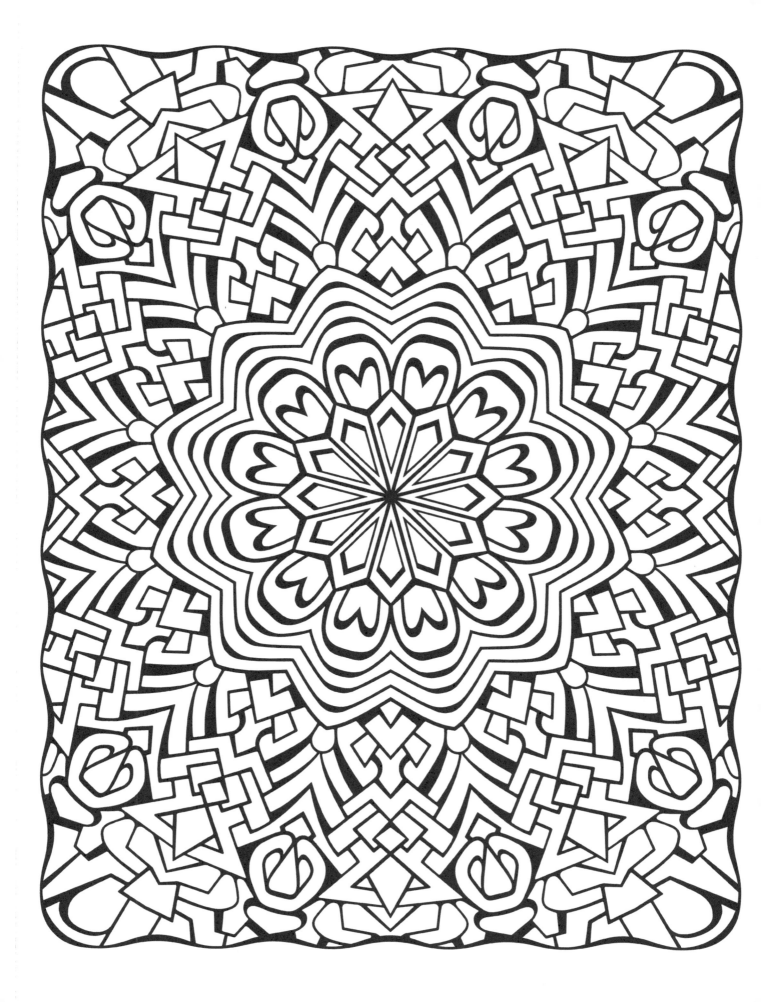

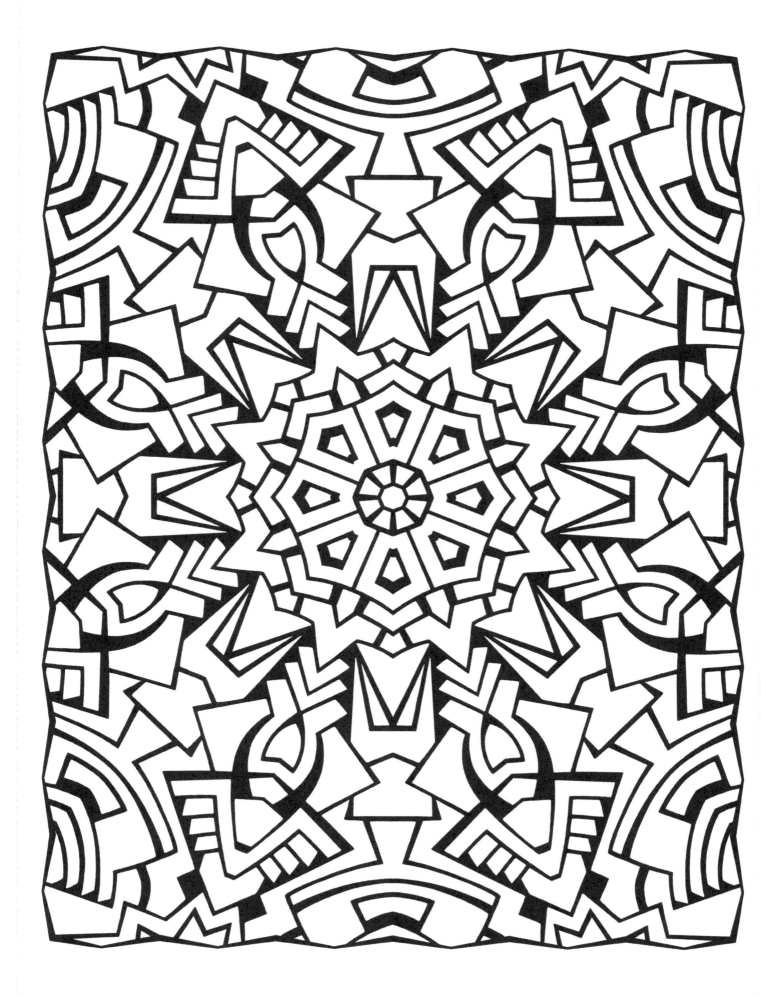

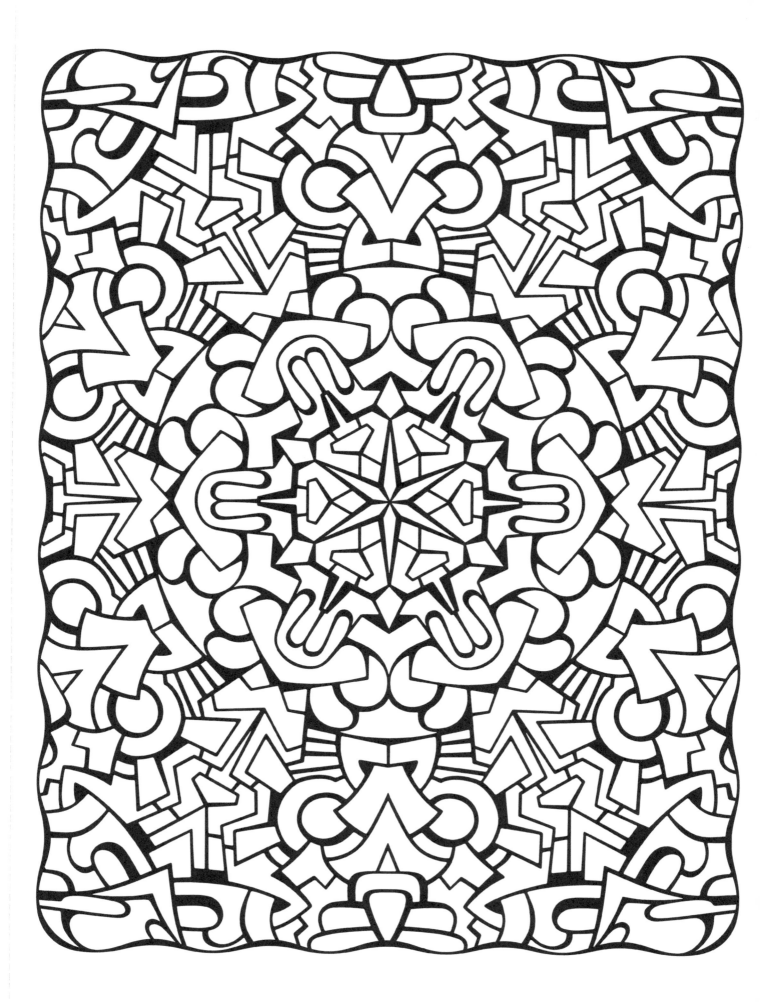

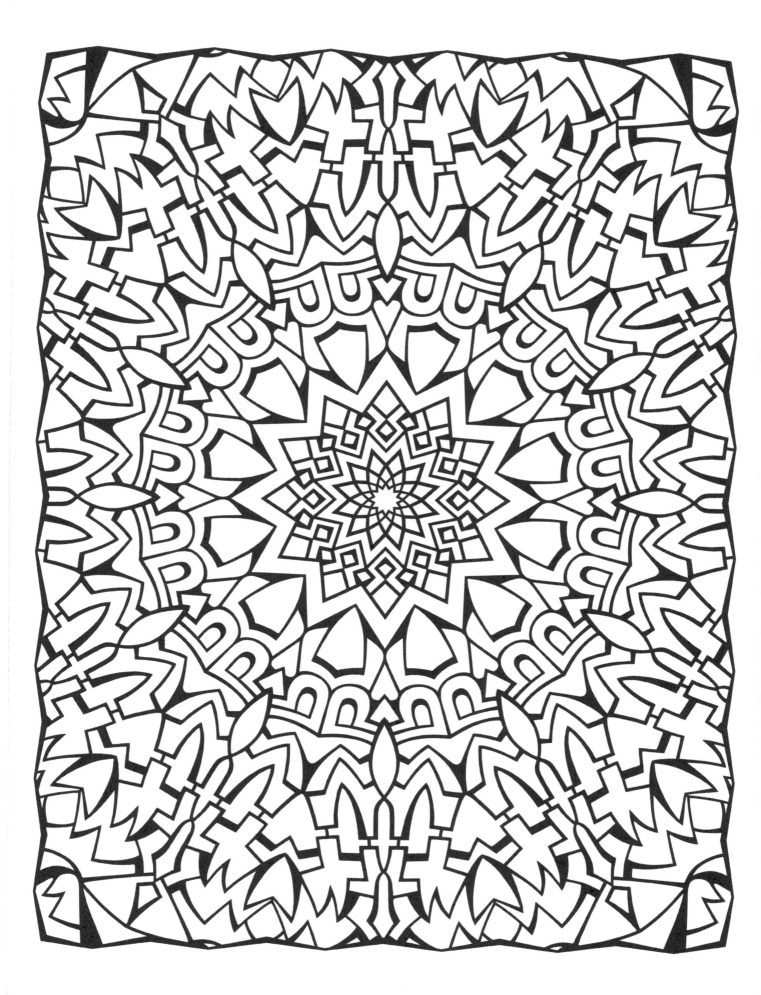

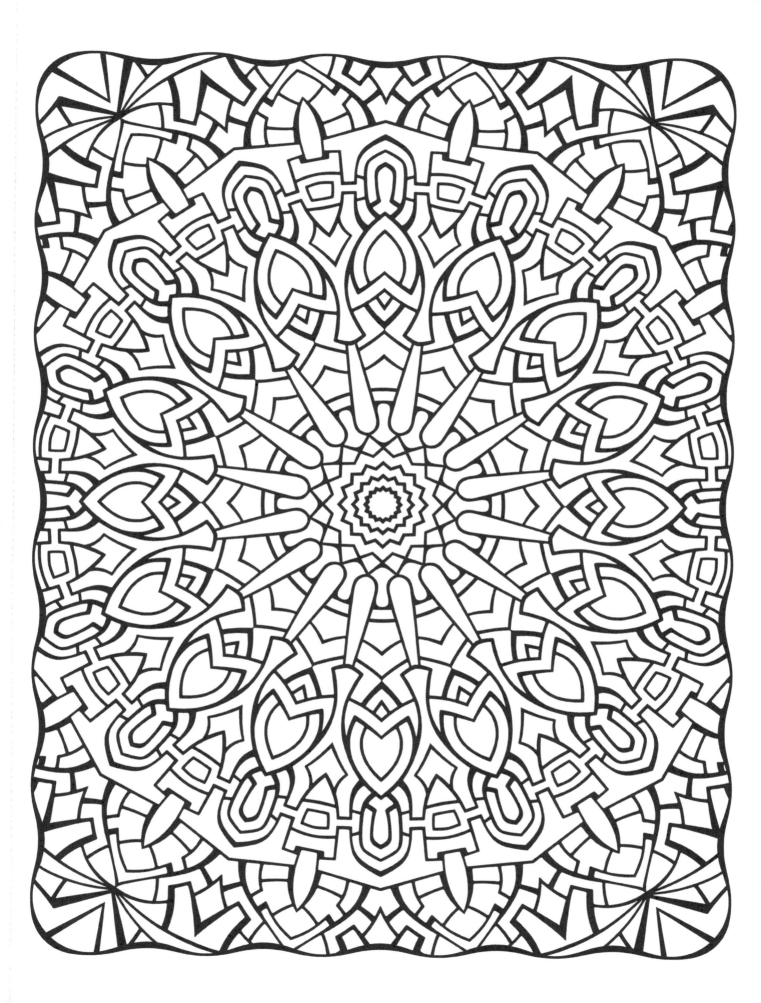

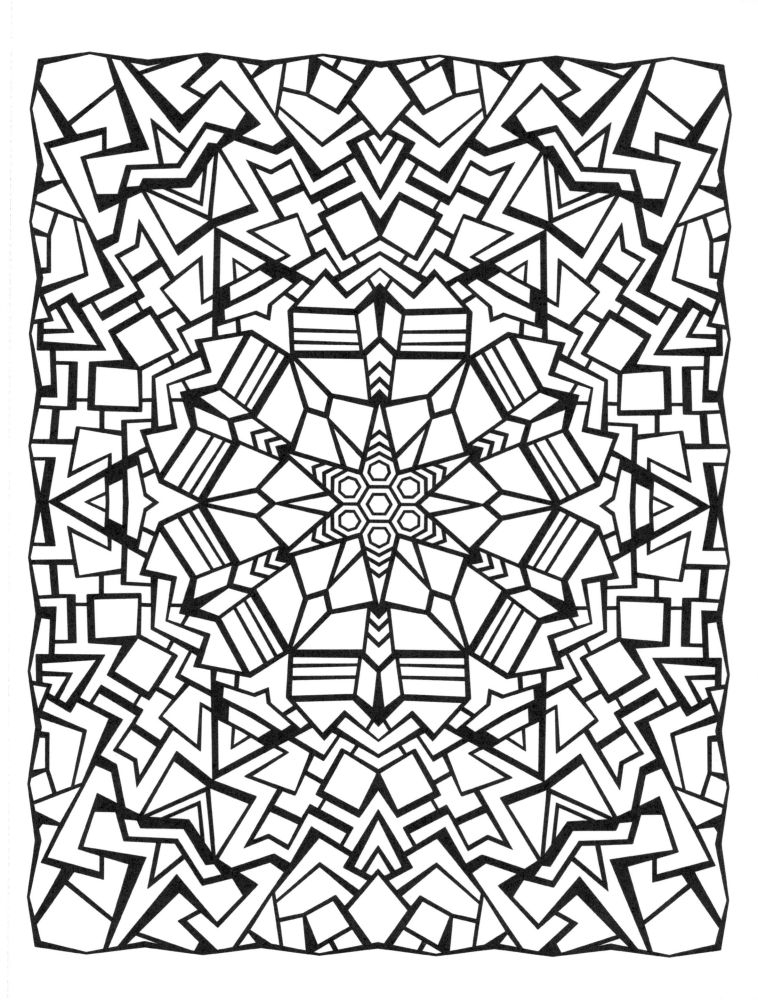

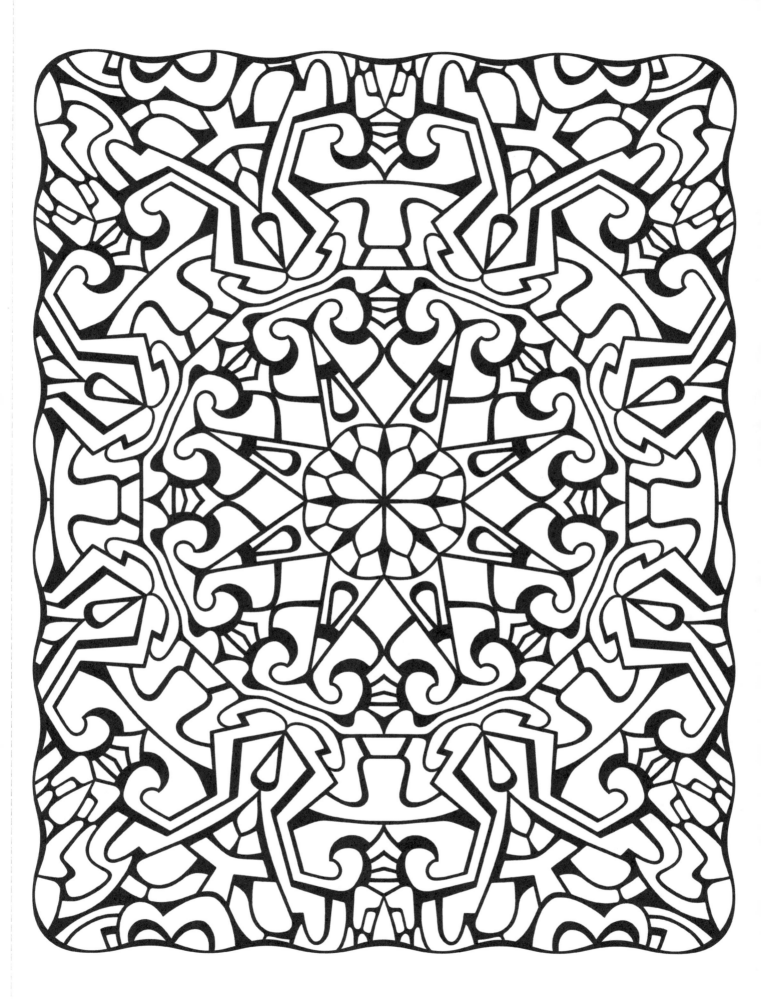

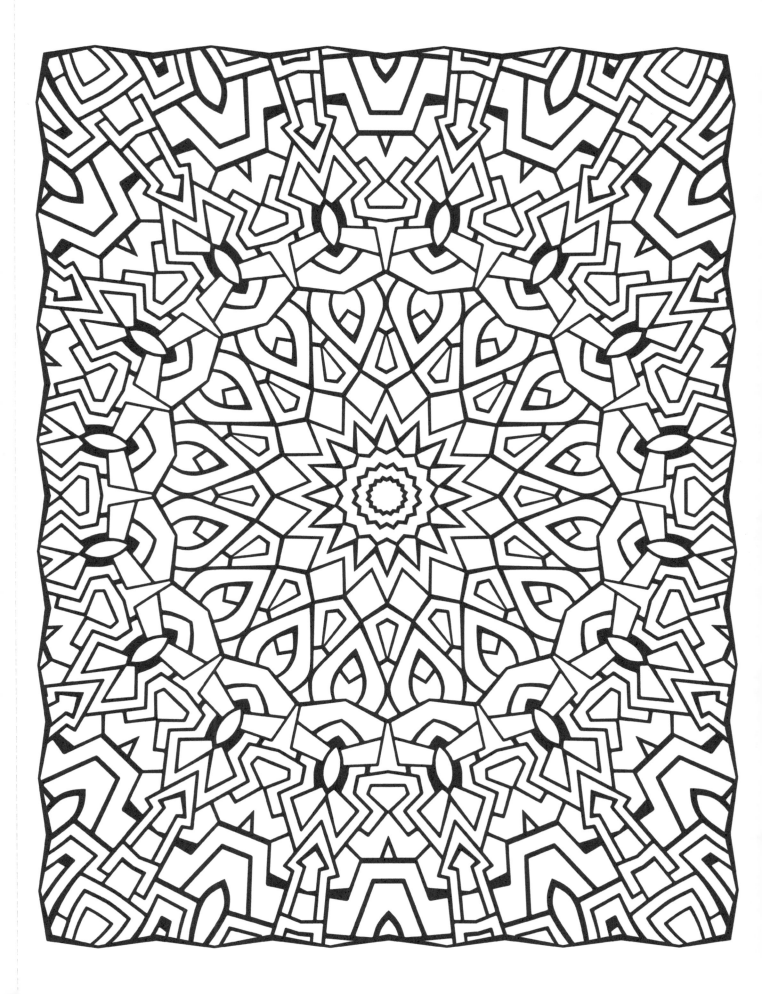

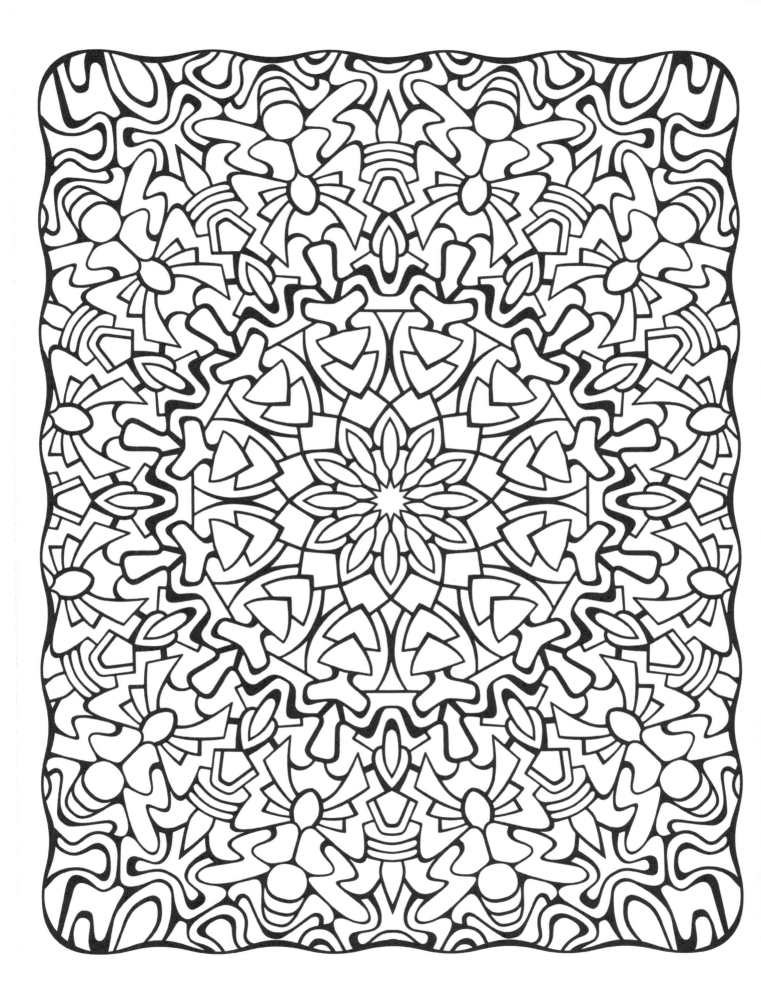

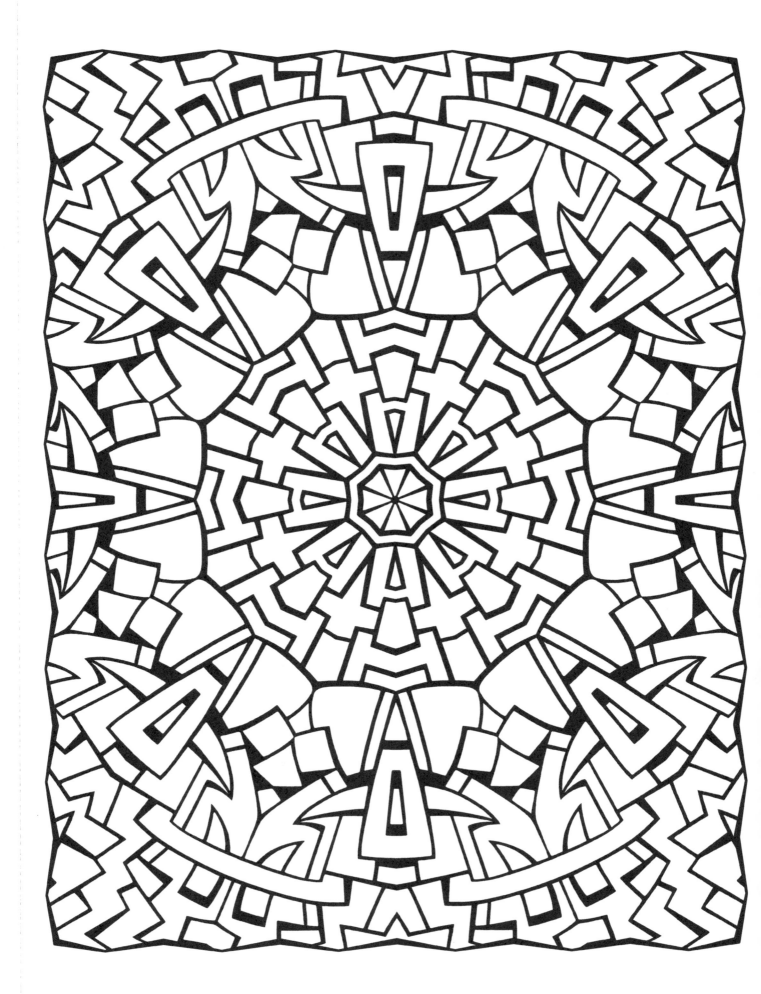

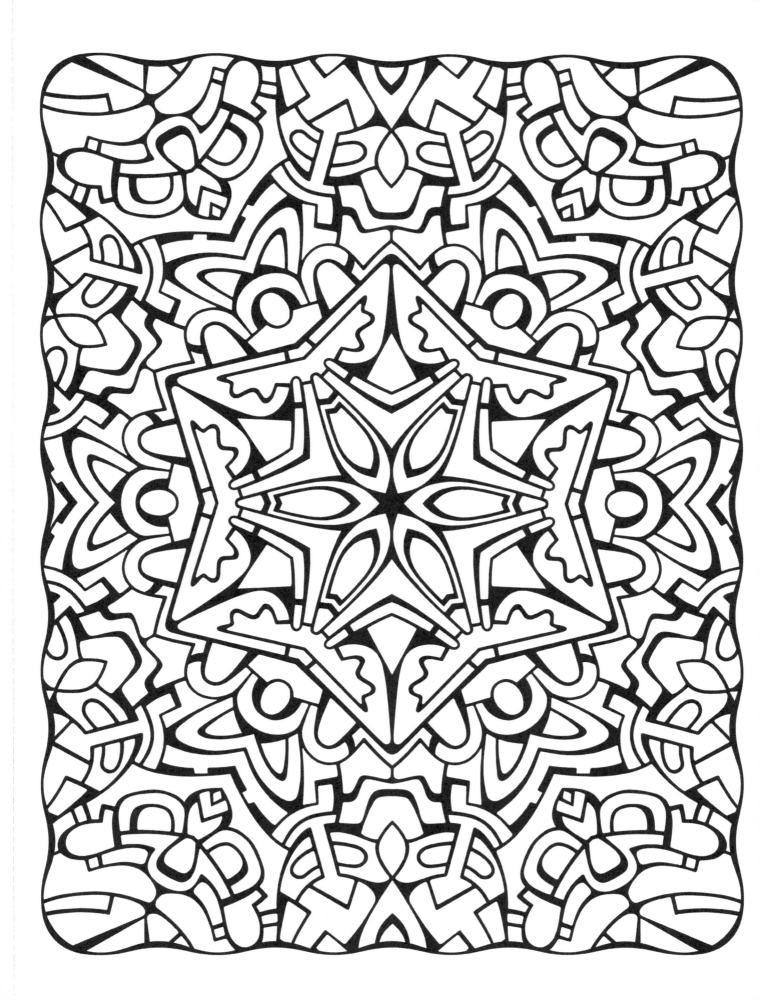

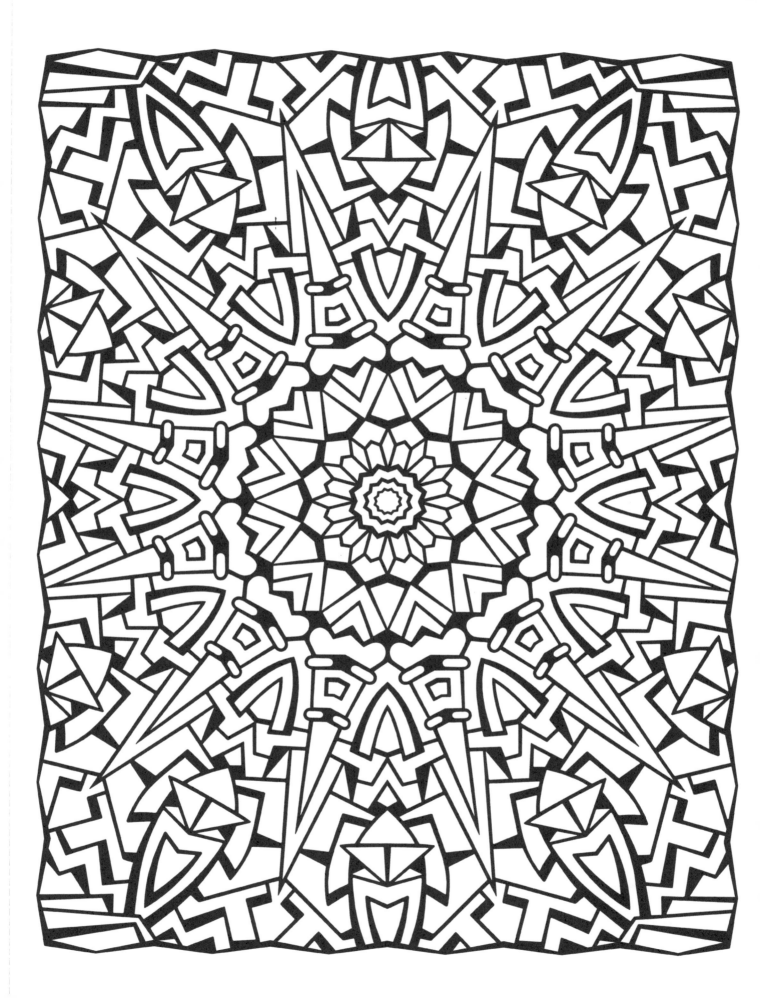

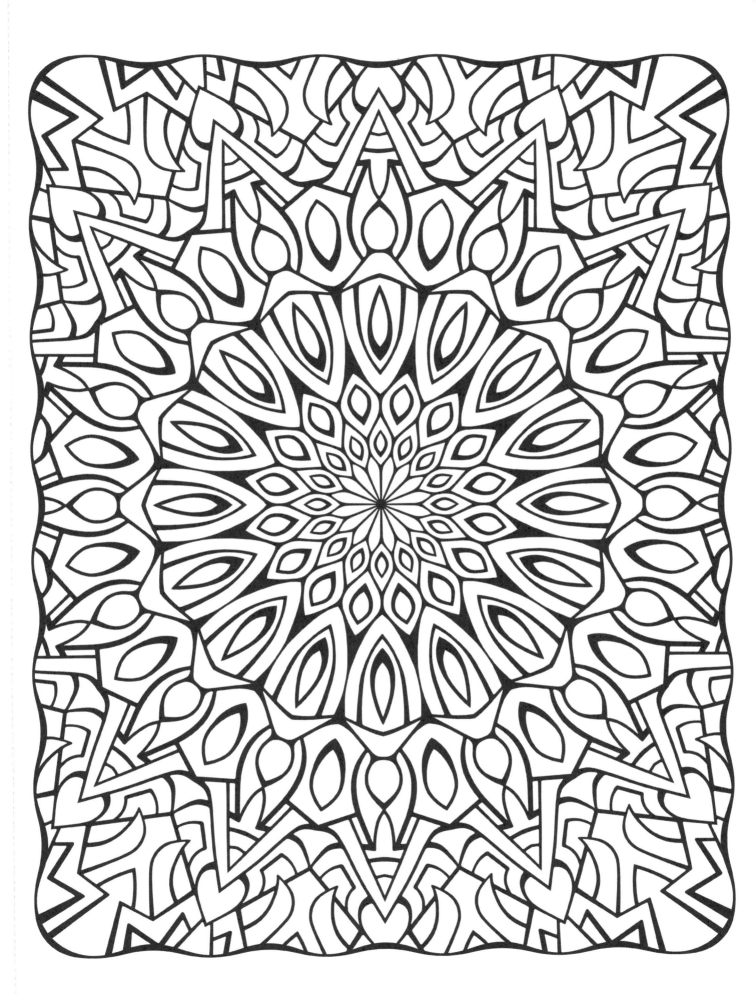